P9-BZQ-800

Pursenalities

20 GREAT KNITTED AND FELTED BAGS

EVA WIECHMANN

Martingale®
& COMPANY

Pursenalities: 20 Great Knitted and Felted Bags
© 2004 by Eva Wiechmann

Martingale & Company
20205 144th Avenue NE
Woodinville, WA 98072-8478 USA
www.martingale-pub.com

Printed in China
09 08 07 06 05 04   8 7 6 5 4 3 2

Credits

President	NANCY J. MARTIN
CEO	DANIEL J. MARTIN
Publisher	JANE HAMADA
Editorial Director	MARY V. GREEN
Managing Editor	TINA COOK
Technical Editor	URSULA REIKES
Copy Editor	LIZ McGEHEE
Design Director	STAN GREEN
Illustrator	ROBIN STROBEL
Cover & Text Designer	TRINA STAHL
Photographer	BRENT KANE

No part of this product may be reproduced in any form, unless otherwise stated, in which case reproduction is limited to the use of the purchaser. The written instructions, photographs, designs, projects, and patterns are intended for the personal, noncommercial use of the retail purchaser and are under federal copyright laws; they are not to be reproduced by any electronic, mechanical, or other means, including informational storage or retrieval systems, for commercial use. Permission is granted to photocopy patterns for the personal use of the retail purchaser.

The information in this book is presented in good faith, but no warranty is given nor results guaranteed. Since Martingale & Company has no control over choice of materials or procedures, the company assumes no responsibility for the use of this information.

MISSION STATEMENT

Dedicated to providing quality products and service to inspire creativity.

Library of Congress Cataloging-in-Publication Data

Wiechmann, Eva.
   Pursenalities : 20 great knitted and felted bags /
Eva Wiechmann.
     p. cm.
   ISBN 1-56477-565-8
  1. Handbags.   2. Tote bags.   3. Knitting—Patterns.
4. Felting. I. Title.
   TT667.W44 2004
   646.4'8—dc22

                       2004010488

Dedication

To my daughter and my grandchildren

Acknowledgments

Many thanks to my husband for printing and editing the text and pictures—and for putting up with all the "wet dogs" hanging around the patio and the house while I was designing these bags.

Thanks to my friend Beth for coming up with the great title and inspiring me with her bold color choices.

Thanks to my customers, who so gracefully have been trying out my patterns and pointing out all the mistakes in the patterns.

Thanks to all my friends for bringing in new design ideas.

And thanks to Cascade Yarns for their support.

Last but not least, thanks to Martingale & Company for giving me a chance. And special thanks to Terry Martin and Ursula Reikes for helping me.

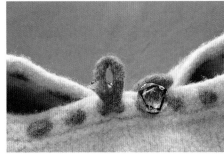

Contents

Introduction

FELTING, JUST like knitting, has experienced a huge comeback in the last couple of years. New knitters like it because the knitting is fast and easy, and it doesn't have to be perfect. "It all comes out in the wash," as I tell the knitters. Experienced knitters love the challenge of experimenting with colors and different textures. They are constantly coming up with new and exciting yarn combinations.

Warning:

This activity may become an addiction, and I don't mind being responsible for it.

In this book, each design has something different to teach you. No two bags are exactly the same. I hope you will enjoy making these bags and totes, and I hope they will inspire you to get creative with different yarns, lots of colors, and new designs. So, go for it, and have fun.

Ladybug bag before and after felting

Getting Started

To MAKE these projects, you need basic knitting supplies and worsted-weight wool that is not a superwash wool, plus a selection of novelty yarns that are used sparingly. You will also need a washing machine. If you have a front-loading washing machine, refer to the manufacturer's instructions for information on how to stop the wash cycle before it gets to the rinse and spin cycles.

Yarn

THE BASIC wool used for all the projects in the book is Cascade 220, a 100% wool that is not a superwash wool. It felts perfectly and comes in many, many beautiful colors—you will feel like a kid in a candy store trying to choose colors. You can substitute any 100% worsted-weight wool that is not a superwash.

Two strands of worsted-weight wool are used throughout, unless the second yarn—a novelty yarn used for texture and fun—has at least 30% wool in it. If there is enough wool in the novelty yarn, then you can use one strand of wool and one strand of novelty yarn. There are a variety of novelty yarns you can use: eyelash, hairy, knobby, variegated, tweed, mohair, and metallic. When trying a new yarn combination that you are not sure of, make a test piece first and felt it. This will prevent wasting time and money on a whole bag if it does not work out to your liking.

Beware that some colors felt better than others. Dark colors felt faster than light colors. White takes a long time to felt, so be careful in using it; off-white is a better choice.

Felting

THIS IS the part that scares most of the "first timers." It is actually very easy to do; just follow the directions below.

1. Put your unfelted bag in a mesh garment bag or a zippered pillowcase.

2. Set up your washing machine for the regular cycle and use hot water. Use a non-rinse wool wash, such as Eucalan; it helps the felting process and smells better than the wet-dog odor you usually get from wet wool. Agitate the bag in the wash cycle *only*; do not let the machine go into the rinse and spin cycles.

   Note: *When felting a bag with lots of colors or lights and darks combined, throw in a Shout Color Catcher sheet. It will trap some of the loose dyes.*

3. Check the progress frequently. Shape and reshape while you are felting to achieve the results you want. To do this, stop the machine and pull the bag out of the water. Pull the handles straight, the corners even, and pull in the length or width of the bag as needed to attain the desired shape.

4. Felt long enough to create a firm fabric (stitches should not be visible anymore). This may require you to reset the machine to the wash cycle more than once. When felting is completed, remember not to let the machine go into the spin and rinse cycles or you will create creases in the bag that are very difficult, if not impossible, to remove. Also, do not let the bag stand in water without agitation. If you do, it may result in discoloration.

5. Squeeze some of the water out by hand. Put the bag between towels and step on it to squeeze out most of the water.

6. Shape again. Pull hard in the desired direction. Put pieces of cardboard in the bottom and sides, or stuff the bag with blank paper to keep the shape while drying.

7. Air-dry the bag. On a sunny day, hang it by the handles out in the open. While the bag is drying, keep shaping it to make sure it comes out the way you want it, and let dry completely.

8. Shave the bag! Yes, you read that correctly. Shave the bag with a razor blade or with a garment shaver if the colors seem to be bleeding or if the edges between two colors are not as clean as you would like them. Shaving makes the colors crisp again.

Finished Sizes after Felting

ALL MEASUREMENTS are approximate. Finished sizes after felting will depend on your choice of yarns, the yarn combinations, the colors, and how tightly or loosely you knit. Don't be too uptight about the size or shape; give each bag a chance to become your own unique design. You can control the size by felting the bag a little more or a little less as desired. Sometimes it looks like all is lost, but remember that a bag can be stretched quite a bit by pulling in the desired direction. Ask for help from someone with strong hands if you cannot do it yourself.

Knitting Basics

*J*UST A few simple techniques are all you need to make the projects in this book.

Gauge

GAUGE IS not too important when making these purses. An approximate gauge of 2 to 2½ stitches per inch is fine. Loose is better than too tight!

Stitches

SIMPLE, BASIC stitch patterns are used for the projects. Note that they are worked differently, depending on whether you are working back and forth or in the round.

Garter Stitch
Worked back and forth: Knit every row.
Worked in the round: Knit 1 round, purl 1 round.

Stockinette Stitch
Worked back and forth: Knit 1 row, purl 1 row.
Worked in the round: Knit every round.

Reverse Stockinette Stitch
Worked back and forth: Purl 1 row, knit 1 row.
Worked in the round: Purl every round.

Seed Stitch
Worked back and forth or in the round:
Row 1: *K1, P1, rep from * across or around.
Row 2: Knit the purl sts and purl the knit sts.
Repeat row 2.

Increases
Increase (Inc)
Knit into front and back of same stitch.

Make 1 (M1)
Pick up horizontal thread between 2 stitches and knit into back of it.

Circular Knitting
Cast on the required number of stitches onto circular needles. To join the round, simply work into the first cast-on stitch and continue around. Make sure the cast-on stitches are not twisted.

Handles

THREE TECHNIQUES are used to make the handles for the bags. Pattern directions indicate where to place handles on each bag and whether to sew them onto the bag or insert them into the knitted pieces. To sew handles, use 2 strands of yarn and a whipstitch. To insert handles, push the end of a handle between 2 stitches at the appropriate place and tie an overhand knot at the end.

I-Cord Handle
With double-pointed needles (dpn), cast on the required number of stitches (as indicated in the pattern). *Do not turn.* Push stitches to the opposite end of the needle and knit across. Repeat until you have the length needed for handles. Bind off.

Join ends of handles by weaving the cast-on end to the bound-off stitches. With yarn, insert the yarn needle inside the cast-on edge and then into the corresponding stitch on the bound-off edge. Continue around.

Flat Handle with Rounded Edges
With straight needles, cast on 5 stitches, turn, *knit 3, slip 2 with yarn in front purlwise, turn. Repeat from * to desired length. Bind off.

OR

With straight needles, cast on 7 stitches, turn, *knit 4, with yarn in front slip 3 stitches purlwise, turn. Repeat from * to desired length. Bind off.

Twisted Cord
For each twisted cord, you'll need 3 strands of wool approximately 3 times the desired length of the twisted cord. Have someone hold one end of 3 strands of wool together (or knot the ends together and hook them on a doorknob) while you twist them until the cord starts to curl when you release tension. Fold the cord in half at the center and let the 2 halves twist together. Tie an overhand knot at each end of the twisted cord.

One-Row Buttonholes

KNIT TO buttonhole placement. *With yarn in front, slip the next 2 stitches purlwise, bind off 1 stitch, with yarn in front slip the next stitch purlwise, and bind off. Repeat as many times as needed for the desired-size buttonhole. Slide last stitch back to left-hand needle, turn, needle cast on (see "Needle Cast On" on page 11) the amount of stitches you bound off, turn. Knit to next buttonhole placement and repeat from * for desired number of buttonholes.

Seams

JOIN SEAMS using a whipstitch and a double strand of worsted-weight wool to ensure even felting.

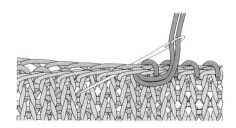

Whipstitch

An exception to this is the Banana Hobo Bag on page 45, where one end of the handle is sewn to the bag with a yarn needle using a Kitchener stitch. With the same number of stitches on 2 needles, and wrong sides together, work stitches together as follows:

1. Go through first stitch on front needle purlwise; leave stitch on needle.

2. Go through first stitch on back needle knitwise; leave stitch on needle.

3. Go through first stitch on front needle knitwise and drop this stitch off the needle. Go through next stitch on front needle purlwise, leave on needle.

4. Go through first stitch on back needle purlwise and drop this stitch off the needle. Go through next stitch on back needle knitwise, leave on needle.

5. Repeat steps 3 through 4 until there is 1 stitch on each needle.

6. Go through remaining stitch on front needle knitwise and drop stitch off.

7. Go through remaining stitch on back needle purlwise and drop stitch off.

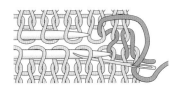

Pockets

POCKETS ARE felted separately and sewn on after all pieces are completely dry. Use perle cotton and a blanket stitch to sew the pocket to the bag. Perle cotton is strong and comes in many colors to match the bag.

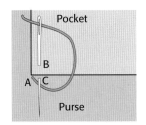

Blanket Stitch

Three-Needle Bind Off

THIS TECHNIQUE is used to join the bottom edges in some of the bags. Divide stitches evenly onto 2 needles and hold with right sides together. With a third needle, knit together 1 stitch from the front needle and 1 stitch from the back needle. *Knit together the next stitch on front and back needles. With 2 stitches on the right needle, bind off by pulling the second stitch over the first stitch and off the needle. Repeat from * until all stitches are bound off.

Knit together one stitch from front needle and one stitch from back needle.

Bind off.

Needle Cast On

*KNIT INTO the stitch on the left needle; do not take it off the needle. Put the new stitch back on the left needle. Repeat from * for the required number of stitches.

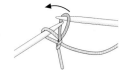

Knit into stitch.

Place new stitch on left needle.

Single Crochet

WORK FROM right to left with the right side of the knitting facing you. Insert hook into knitting stitch, yarn over hook, pull loop of yarn through the knitting to the front, yarn over hook, and pull it through the first loop. *Insert hook into next stitch of knitting, yarn over hook, pull loop of yarn through stitch, yarn over hook, and pull through both loops on hook. Repeat from * to end.

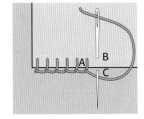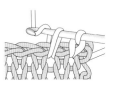

Insert hook into stitch, yarn over hook, pull loop through to front, yarn over hook.

Pull loop through both loops on hook.

Americana Tote

Go red, white, and blue with this star-spangled bag!

Materials

- Cascade 220 (100% wool; 220 yards) in the following amounts and colors:
  - 2 (3, 3) skeins of Blue
  - 1 (2, 2) skeins each of White and Red
- Size 15 US (10 mm) circular needles (29")
- Size 11 US (8 mm) needles
- 1 skein of perle cotton for star

Bag

BEG BAG at bottom. Work 2 strands of yarn held together throughout.

- With size 15 needles and Blue, CO 80 (90,120) sts and join into rnd. Knit 6 (8, 10) rnds.
- Purl 1 rnd.
- Work Red and White stripes as follows:
  - With Red, knit 4 (6, 6) rnds.
  - With White, knit 4 (6, 6) rnds.
  - Rep above Red and White stripes 2 (3, 4) times.
- With Red, knit 4 (6, 6) rnds.
- With Blue, knit for 5".
- **Dec rnd:** (K8, K2tog) around—72 (81, 108) sts. Work 4 (6, 8) rnds in garter st (see page 9). BO all sts pw.

Star

WITH size 11 needles and White, CO 20 sts. Work 5" in St st.

Handles (Make 2)

WITH SIZE 11 needles and Blue, CO 7 sts, turn, *K4, wyif sl 3 sts pw, turn, rep from * for 18 (20, 22)".

Finishing

- With WS tog, sew bottom seam with whipstitch. To make bottom corner gusset, turn bag inside out, and fold and stitch corners with yarn as shown.

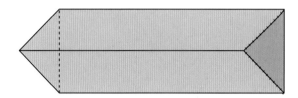

- Referring to photo, sew handles to top edge approximately 4" from corner.
- Referring to directions on page 8, felt the bag and white piece at the same time.
- Cut out star and sew to front of bag with perle cotton and a blanket st (see page 11).

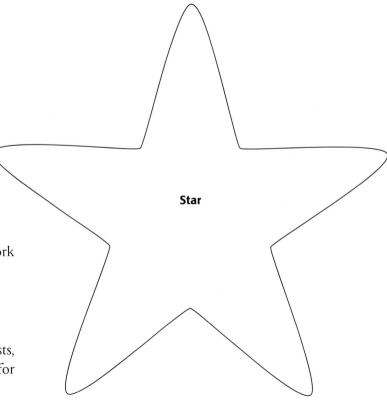

Star

Vintage Bubble Bag

This bubble bag reminds me of my mom's shopping bag—roomy and practical. This vintage look is very stylish right now, and although I used colors that are subtle, you can make yours wild and bold.

Materials

- **MC** 2 skeins of Cascade 220 (100% wool; 220 yards), Gray
- **CC** 2 skeins of Noro Silk Garden (45% silk, 45% mohair, 10% lamb's wool; 110 yards), color to coordinate with MC
- Size 15 US (10 mm) circular needles (24")
- Size 10½ US (6.5 mm) circular needles (24")
- Size 10½ US (6.5 mm) dpn

Bag   *Knit a row - Purl a row*

BEG BAG at top. Work 2 strands of yarn held tog throughout.

- With size 10½ circular needles and 1 strand each of MC and CC held tog, CO 68 sts and join into rnd. Work 14 rnds in garter st (see page 9).
- **Dec rnd:** (K1, K2tog) around to last 2 sts, end K2tog—45 sts.
- Inc by knitting into front and back of every st—(90 sts).
- Change to size 15 circular needles and knit until piece measures 12" from beg.
- **Beg dec rnds:**
  - (K7, K2tog) around—(80 sts). Knit 4 rnds even.
  - (K6, K2tog) around—(70 sts). Knit 3 rnds even.
  - (K5, K2tog) around—(60 sts). Knit 2 rnds even.
  - (K4, K2tog) around—(50 sts). Knit 1 rnd.
- With RS tog, join bottom with 3-needle BO (see page 11).

Handles (Make 2)

WITH dpn and MC, work 5-st I-cord for 20" (see page 10).

Finishing

- Sew each end of a handle to top edge approx 1½" from each corner. Rep with second handle on opposite side.
- Referring to directions on page 8, felt the bag.

Handles sewn to top edge of bag

on row 7
handles
openings
K6 - bind off 2
K18 - bind off 2
K12 - bind off 2
K18 - bind off 2
on row 8 K around
cast on 2
where you had
cast off

Not-So-Vintage Bubble Bag

*The sedate Vintage Bubble Bag is reinvented with funky yarns
and different handles.*

Materials

- **A**   2 skeins of Cascade 220 (100% wool; 220 yards), Dark Gray
- **B**   2 skeins of Berroco Hip Hop (100% thick-and-thin wool; 76 yards), Gray Multi
- **C**   1 skein of Berroco Zap (100% poly-ester; 50 yards), Gray Multi
- Size 13 US (9 mm) circular needles (24")
- Size 11 US (8 mm) dpn
- 1 button, 1" diameter

Bag

BEG BAG at top. Work 2 strands of yarn held tog throughout unless otherwise indicated.

- With size 13 needles and A, CO 68 sts and join into rnd. Work 10 rnds in garter st (see page 9).
- Change to 1 strand of B (if you use A throughout, cont with 2 strands). **Dec rnd:** (K1, K2tog) around to last 2 sts, end K2tog—45 sts.
- Inc by knitting in front and back of every st—90 sts.
- Add 1 strand of C to 1 strand of B for 4 rnds. Cut C.
- Cont with B (or 2 strands of A); knit until piece measures 12" from beg.
- **Dec rnds:**
  - (K7, K2 tog) around—80 sts. Knit 3 rnds even.
  - (K6, K2 tog) around—70 sts. Knit 2 rnds even.
- Change to 2 strands of A and work 4 rnds in garter st.
- With RS tog, join bottom with 3-needle BO (see page 11).

Handles

- With dpn and A, work 4-st I-cord for 36" (see page 10).

Finishing

- Starting at outside front of bag, insert end of handle between first and second garter ridge, approx 4 sts from side. Pull end through bag and out the back at same point; rep at opposite side. Join ends tog (see page 10).
- Make a 3-st I-cord about 4" long for button loop. Join ends tog and sew to center of back at top edge.
- Referring to directions on page 8, felt the bag.
- Sew button on opposite side to correspond with button loop.

Inserted handles at side edge (above), button loop (below)

Spring Fling Bag

*This flirty, wild bag is based on the Vintage Bubble Bag—
but larger and with a closure.*

Materials

- **MC**   3 skeins of Cascade 220 (100% wool; 220 yards), Light Heather Green
- **CC**   2 balls of Crystal Palace Fizz (100% polyester; 120 yards), color to coordinate with MC
- Size 10½ US (6.5 mm) circular needles (24")
- Size 15 US (10 mm) circular needles (24")
- Size 11 US (8 mm) dpn
- 3 buttons, ⅝" diameter

Bag

BEG BAG at top. Work 2 strands of yarn held tog throughout unless otherwise indicated.

- With size 10½ needles and MC, CO 68 sts and join into rnd. Work 14 rnds in garter st (see page 9).
- **Dec rnd:** (K1, K2tog) around to last 2 sts, end K2tog—45 sts.
- Inc by knitting into front and back of every st—90 sts.
- Change to size 15 needles, add 1 strand of CC to 2 strands of MC and knit until piece measures 13" from beg.
- **Dec rnds:**
  - (K7, K2tog) around—80 sts. Knit 4 rnds even.
  - (K6, K2tog) around—70 sts. Knit 3 rnds even.
  - (K5, K2tog) around—60 sts. Knit 2 rnds even.
  - (K4, K2tog) around—50 sts. Knit 1 rnd.
- With RS tog, join bottom with 3-needle BO (see page 11).

Flap

- With RS facing, size 15 needles, and MC, PU 28 sts from back top edge. Work 10 rows in garter st.
- **Next row:** Work 3 buttonholes as follows: K4, (BO 4, K4) 3 times (see "One-Row Buttonholes" on page 10).
- Knit 1 row.
- Knit 2 rows, dec 1 st at beg and end of each row. BO all sts kw.

Handles (Make 2)

WITH dpn and MC, CO 4 sts and work I-cord for 23" (see page 10).

Finishing

- Insert ends of handles from the inside between third and fourth row from top, approx 4 sts from each side. Knot ends of handles on the outside of the bag.
- Referring to directions on page 8, felt the bag.
- Sew on buttons to correspond with buttonholes.

Handles knotted at ends

Blue Hawaii Tote

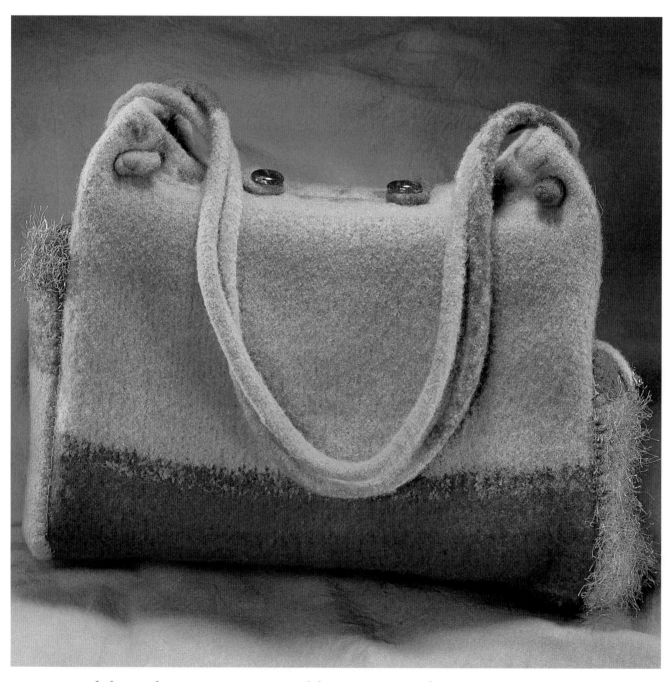

Aloha! This tote was inspired by Maui, my favorite vacation spot.
When I carry this tote, I can almost smell the plumeria and hear the ocean.

Materials

- Cascade 220 (100% wool; 220 yards) in the following amounts and colors:
  - A   2 skeins of Royal Blue
  - B   1 skein of French Blue
  - C   1 skein of Kelly Green
  - D   1 skein of Jade
  - E   1 skein of Turquoise
  - F   1 skein of Sky Blue
  - G   1 skein of Light Blue
- 1 ball of Crystal Palace Fizz (100% polyester; 120 yards), Blue
- Size 15 US (10 mm) circular needles (29")
- Size 11 US (8 mm) dpn
- Stitch markers
- 3 buttons, ⅞" diameter
- 1 skein of perle cotton for pockets

Bag

BEG AT bottom. Work 2 strands of yarn held tog throughout.

- With size 15 needles and color A, CO 130 sts and join into rnd. Knit 12 rnds. Purl 1 rnd.
- **Next rnd:** K7, PM, wyib sl 1 pw, K49, PM, wyib sl 1 pw, K14, PM, wyib sl 1 pw, K49, PM, wyib sl 1 pw, K7.
- **Next rnd:** Knit without slipping stitches.

- Rep last 2 rnds until piece measures 20", following the color sequence below:
  - 6 rnds with 2 strands of A
  - 4 rnds with 1 strand each of A and B
  - 6 rnds with 2 strands of B
  - 4 rnds with 1 strand each of B and C
  - 6 rnds with 2 strands of C
  - 4 rnds with 1 strand each of C and D
  - 6 rnds with 2 strands of D
  - 4 rnds with 1 strand each of D and E
  - 6 rnds with 2 strands of E
  - 4 rnds with 1 strand each of E and F
  - 6 rnds with 2 strands of F
  - 4 rnds with 1 strand each of F and G
- **Dec rnd:** Cont in G, (K8, K2tog) around— 117 sts.
- Work 8 rnds in garter st (see page 9). BO all sts pw.

Handles (Make 2)

WITH dpn and 2 strands of any color wool, work 5-st I-cord for 42" (see page 10). I changed yarn colors about every 7", following a color sequence similar to the tote with remaining colors.

Top Edge

- With dpn and 2 strands of any color wool, work 3-st I-cord long enough to reach all around top of bag plus an extra 8" (4" for each of 2 button loops).
- Make 1 more 3-st I-cord, 5" long, for side-pocket button loop.

Handles knotted at ends

Button loops

Pockets

FOR EACH pocket, use size 15 needles and 2 strands of any color wool, adding 1 strand of Fizz as desired. Make 2 pockets, one about 11" long and another about 8" long. CO 16 sts and work in St st, ending with 6 rows of garter st. BO all sts.

Finishing

- With WS tog, sew bottom seam with whip-stitch.
- Turn bag inside out. Fold and sew bottom corners, using purl row as guideline (see page 13 for making bottom gusset).
- Insert each end of a handle about 4 sts from corners and below garter-st edge, going in from the sides and out the fronts. Knot ends of handle on outside of bag. Rep with second handle on opposite side.

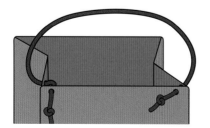

Insert ends of handle
at each side of front.

- Weave I-cord for top edge in and out every 2 sts between rows 4 and 5 of garter-st edge. Make 2 button loops by pulling about 4" of I-cord toward outside of back, approx one-third the distance from each corner. Join ends of I-cord tog (see page 10).
- Pull short I-cord through side of bag at center, 9" from bottom, and join ends tog inside bag.
- Referring to directions on page 8, felt the bag and pockets.
- Sew pockets in place with perle cotton using a blanket st.
- Sew on buttons to correspond with button loops.

My home country, Finland, has beautiful sunsets, but the ones in my current home of Southern California are simply stunning. The multitude of colors never ceases to amaze me. These colors inspired my backyard garden—and this tote.

Materials

- Cascade 220 (100% wool; 220 yards) in the following amounts and colors:
  - **A**   2 skeins of Hot Pink
  - **B**   1 skein of Purple
  - **C**   1 skein of Rose
  - **D**   1 skein of Dark Orange
  - **E**   1 skein of Light Orange
  - **F**   1 skein of Dark Yellow
  - **G**   1 skein of Light Yellow
- 1 ball of Crystal Palace Fizz (100% polyester; 120 yards), Red
- 1 ball of Crystal Palace Fizz (100% polyester; 120 yards), Yellow
- Size 15 US (10 mm) circular needles (29")
- Size 11 US (8 mm) dpn
- Stitch markers
- 2 buttons, 1" diameter
- 1 skein of perle cotton for pockets

Bag

BEG AT bottom. Work 2 strands of yarn held tog throughout.

- With size 15 needles and A, cast on 51 sts. Knit 1 row.
- Work 16 rows in seed st (see page 9).
- Purl 1 row.
- Needle CO 79 sts (see "Needle Cast On" on page 11) and join into rnd—130 sts. Purl 1 rnd.
- **Next rnd:** Starting on long side of bottom piece, K50, PM, K15, PM, K50, PM, K15, PM.

- **Next rnd:** Knit to first marker, slip marker, *sl 1 st after marker and knit to next marker. Rep from * around.
- Rep last 2 rnds until piece measures 20" from needle CO, following the color sequence below:
  - 4 rnds with 2 strands of A
  - 4 rnds with 1 strand each of A and B
  - 8 rnds with 2 strands of B
  - 4 rnds with 1 strand each of B and C
  - 6 rnds with 2 strands of C
  - 4 rnds with 1 strand each of C and D
  - 6 rnds with 2 strands of D
  - 4 rnds with 1 strand each of D and E
  - 6 rnds with 2 strands of E
  - 4 rnds with 1 strand each of E and F
  - 6 rnds with 2 strands of F
  - 4 rnds with 1 strand each of F and G
  - 6 rnds with 2 strands of G
- **Dec rnd:** Cont with G, (K8, K2 tog) around—117 sts.
- Work 8 rnds in garter st (see page 9). BO all sts pw.

Handles (Make 2)

WITH dpn and 2 strands of any color yarn, work 5-st I-cord for 36" (see page 10). I changed yarn colors about every 6", following a color sequence similar to the tote.

Pockets

FOR EACH pocket, use size 15 needles and 2 strands of any color yarn, adding 1 strand of Fizz as desired. Make 2 pockets, one about 11" long and another about 8" long. CO 14 sts and work in St st, ending with 6 rows of garter st. BO all sts.

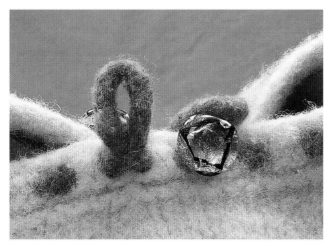

Button loops

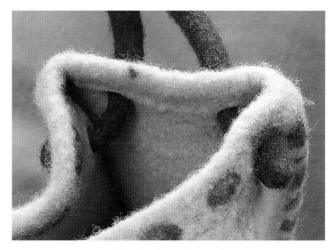

Handles knotted at ends

Twisted Cord Trim (Make 2)

MAKE TWISTED cord (see page 10). Make a knot in one end of twisted cord. Starting at bottom of one side and working up to the top, weave cord around slipped sts, then in and out of every 2 sts across top of bag, leaving one button loop about 5" long (placed slightly offset). Cont down other side; knot end of cord. Rep for other side, making a second 5" long button loop. One button will close toward front and other toward back.

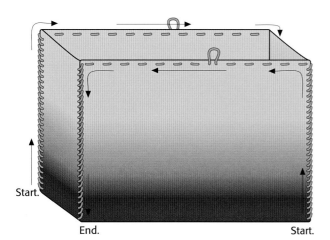

Finishing

- With WS tog, sew bottom to CO sts with whipstitch.
- Insert each end of a handle about 4 sts from corners and just below garter-st ridge, going in from the sides and out the fronts. Knot ends of handle on outside of bag. Rep with second handle on opposite side.
- Referring to directions on page 8, felt the bag.
- Sew on pockets with perle cotton using a blanket st.
- Sew buttons at top edge on opposite sides to correspond with button loops.

Summer in the City Tote

*A beautiful beaded bag I saw in a fashion magazine was the inspiration
for this tote. Of course, I just had to see if my version could be felted,
and I'm thrilled with the result.*

Materials

- 1 skein of Cascade 220 (100% wool; 220 yards) in each of the following colors:
  - A   Kelly Green
  - B   Light Heather Green
  - C   Off-White
  - D   Light Blue
  - E   White
  - F   Medium Sky Blue
- Size 15 US (10 mm) circular needles (24")
- Size 11 US (8 mm) dpn
- Size I crochet hook
- Small amounts of green and red tapestry wool for flowers
- Approx 48 seed beads
- ¾ yard of ¼"-wide satin ribbon

Bag

BEG BAG at bottom. Work 2 strands of yarn held tog throughout.

- With size 15 needles and A, CO 80 sts and join into rnd. Knit 1 rnd.
- **Next rnd:** Inc 1 st in first st and 41st st—82 sts. Knit 1 rnd.
- **Next rnd:** Inc in first 3 sts by knitting in front and back of each st, K38, inc in next 3 sts as before, knit to end of row—88 sts.
- Knit 2 rnds.
- Purl 1 rnd.
- Knit 6 rnds.

- Cont knitting rnds in following color sequence:
  - 6 rnds with 1 strand each of A and C
  - 10 rnds with 1 strand each of C and B
  - 10 rnds with 1 strand each of D and E
  - 10 rnds with 2 strands of D
  - 8 rnds with 1 strand each of D and F
  - 4 rnds with 2 strands of F
- **Dec rnd:** Cont with F, (K9, K2tog) around— 80 sts.
- Work 4 rnds in garter st (see page 9). BO all sts pw.

Handle

WITH dpn and F, work 5-st I-cord for 36" (see page 10).

Finishing

- With WS tog, sew bottom seam with whipstitch.
- To add handle, insert I-cord from the front, approx 3" from side. Thread it through the bag and out the back side as shown; rep at other end of bag and join ends tog (see page 10).

Handle threaded through tote bag at side edge

- With 2 strands of A, sc around bottom once, using purl rnd as guide.
- Embroider 3 flowers on each side of bag with 2 strands of tapestry wool in lazy daisy and stem st.

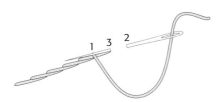

Stem Stitch

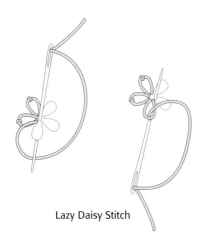

Lazy Daisy Stitch

- Referring to directions on page 8, felt the bag. Move handles back and forth during felting so they don't felt in place.
- Sew 8 beads in center of each flower after felting.
- Referring to photo on page 26, weave satin ribbon through top of bag, below garter st rnds.

Embroidered flowers

Tartan Trend Bag

This bag challenged me to create vertical stripes without carrying multiple yarns.
I also wanted it to look more like a handbag than a tote.
I think the beaded zipper pull gives this bag a touch of class.

Materials

- 2 skeins each of Cascade 220 (100% wool; 220 yards) in Black and Green
- Size 15 US (10 mm) circular needles (24")
- Size 11 (8 mm) dpn
- Size I crochet hook
- Separating zipper (measure for length after bag is felted)
- Sharp needle and sewing thread to match zipper
- Assorted beads for zipper pull
- Short length of perle cotton for zipper pull

Bag

BEG BAG at bottom. Work 2 strands of yarn held tog throughout.

- With size 15 needles and Black, CO 35 sts. Work bottom of purse as follows:
  - Purl 1 row, knit 3 rows, purl 1 row.
  - *With Green, knit 2 rows; then with Black, knit 1 row, purl 1 row. Rep from * once.
  - With Black, knit 2 rows, purl 1 row. This forms bottom of purse.
- With Black, needle CO 59 sts (see "Needle Cast On" on page 11) —94 sts. Join into rnd and purl 1 rnd.
- **Next rnd:** With Green, starting on long side of bottom piece, K35, P12, K35, P12. (Knit sts are front and back of purse, and purl sts are sides).
- Cont in patt for 36 rounds, in random stripes of Black and Green. I know you hate the word random, but really, just do them as you like.

- **Dec rnd:** *K2tog, K31, K2tog, P12, rep from * once. Work dec rnd every other rnd 3 times total, keeping in mind that you have 2 fewer knit sts on each long side with each dec rnd—82 sts.
- Knit 4 rnds even.
- Purl 1 row, binding off 12 side sts on both ends.
- **Flaps:** With Green, work top flap back and forth on 29 sts in St st for 6 rows. BO all sts pw. Rep for flap on opposite side.

Plaid Stripes

FOR VERTICAL stripes, weave 2 strands of Black over 2 sts and under 1 st. Start with 6 rows in center, then evenly space 3 rows on both sides twice. Make sure not to pull yarn too tight.

Handle

WITH dpn and Black, work 3-st I-cord for 42" (see page 10).

Finishing

- With WS tog, sew bottom to CO sts with whipstitch.
- With 2 strands of Black, sc around bag. Start on one side at bottom, work up side, across top flap, and down other side, across bottom of side, and cont around other side, ending at same point you started.

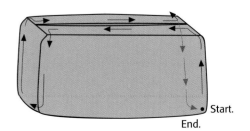

Start.
End.

- Insert handle through sides of purse from inside to outside and then outside to inside about ½" from top edge. Rep for other side and join ends tog (see page 10).

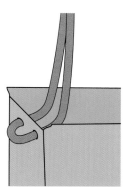

- Referring to directions on page 8, felt the bag.
- Sew in zipper with regular sewing thread and a sharp needle.
- To make zipper pull, thread beads onto perle cotton and knot the ends to hold the beads. Attach to zipper.

Inserted handle at side edge

Beaded zipper pull

Chic Shopping Bag

This is a chic bag for the sophisticated shopper.

FINISHED SIZE AFTER FELTING:
Approx 14" wide x 11" high x 3" deep

Materials

- Cascade 220 (100% wool; 220 yards) in the following amounts and colors:
  - 3 skeins of Black
  - 2 skeins of Gray
  - 1 skein of Red
- 1 ball of Crystal Palace Fizz (100% polyester; 120 yards), Gray
- Size 15 US (10 mm) circular needles (29")
- Size 11 US (8 mm) dpn
- 1 button, 1¼" diameter
- 3 strands of ⅛"-wide Ultrasuede from Rainbow Gallery (I used 2 Red and 1 Black)
- 1 medium-size bead
- 6 purse bottoms. These are brads that protect the bottom of the purse.

Bag

BEG BAG at bottom. Work 2 strands of yarn held tog throughout.

- With size 15 needles and Black, CO 44 sts and work 14 rows in seed st (see page 9).
- Needle CO 68 sts (see "Needle Cast On" on page 11)—112 sts. Join into rnd and purl 1 rnd.
- **Next rnd:** Starting on long side of bottom piece, K44, wyib sl 1 pw, K10, wyib sl 1 pw, K44, wyib sl 1 pw, K10, wyib sl 1 pw.
- **Next rnd:** Knit without slipping sts.
- Rep last 2 rnds, working stripes as follows:
  - (4 rows Gray, 1 row Black) 2 times
  - (3 rows Gray, 1 row Black) 4 times
  - (2 rows Gray, 1 row Black) 2 times
  - (1 row Gray, 1 row Black) 2 times
  - 1 row Gray
  - 4 rows Black
  - 1 row Red
  - 4 rows Black

- (1 row Gray, 1 row Black) 3 times
- 2 rows Gray
- 1 row Black
- Change to Gray and work until piece measures 18" from needle CO.
- **Dec rnd:** (K8, K2tog) around to last 12 sts, end K10, K2tog—(101 sts).
- Add Fizz to the 2 strands of wool and work 6 rnds in garter st (see page 9). BO all sts pw.

Handles (Make 2)

WITH dpn and Black, work 5-st I-cord for 18" (see page 10).

Finishing

- With WS tog, sew bottom seam with whipstitch.
- Starting at top edge about 4" from corner and working toward the bottom of the bag, weave the end of the handle in and out for about 1½". Knot the ends. Rep at each corner. Tack down ends on right side using red yarn.

Weave handles in and out.

- Cut 6 strands of red about 42" long. Fold 3 strands in half and weave around slipped sts for corner pattern, starting about 1½" from top, go down side, across narrow part of bottom edge, and up other side. Rep with rem 3 strands on other side.
- Referring to directions on page 8, felt the bag.
- **Button closure:** Thread 3 strands of Ultrasuede on a blunt needle and take a stitch about ½" long in center of one side, about 1" from top, leaving ends on outside of bag. Pull ends of strands so they are even in length; divide them into 3 groups of 2 strands each and braid them tog. Add a bead at end and tie a knot below bead.

- Sew on button in center of opposite side about 1" from top. To close, wrap braid around button 1 or 2 times.
- Insert prongs on purse bottoms through the bottom fabric of bag from outside to inside, and bend the prongs flat on the inside of the bag (3 on each side).

Button closure

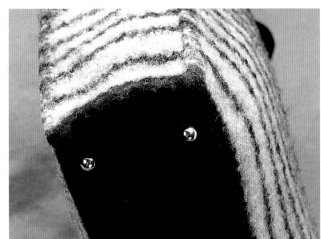

Purse bottoms

Ruffles to Riches Bag

This pattern was based on a designer bag in a European magazine.
I had to make lots of practice ruffles to find the perfect one—kind of like
kissing many frogs to find the prince.

FINISHED SIZE AFTER FELTING:
Approx 14" wide x 9" high

Materials

- Cascade 220 (100% wool; 220 yards) in the following amounts and colors:
  - **MC** 2 skeins of Light Green
  - **CC1** 1 skein of Very Light Green
  - **CC2** 1 skein of Black
- 1 skein of Gedifra Kid Royal (60% super kid mohair, 34% polyamid, 6% wool; 108 yards), color to match Cascade 220 CC1
- Size 11 US (8 mm) circular needles (24")
- Size 15 US (10 mm) circular needles (24")
- Size 17 US (12 mm) circular needles (29")
- Size 10½ (6.5 mm) dpn
- Size F crochet hook
- 2 cards of Rainbow Gallery Very Velvet Petite, color Black (thin velour trim)
- 2 pieces of vinyl tubing 16" long, ⅛" diameter (optional)
- Sharp needle and sewing thread
- 1 button, ¾" diameter

Bag

BEG BAG at bottom. Work 2 strands of yarn held tog throughout unless otherwise indicated.

- With size 15 needles and MC, CO 90 sts and join into rnd. Knit for 13". Leave sts on the needle.
- To make the ruffle, with size 17 needles and 1 strand each of CC1 and Kid Royal held tog, CO 180 sts and join into rnd. Knit 4 rnds. Do not cut the yarns.
- **Dec rnd:** With size 11 needles and *only 1* strand of CC2, knit ruffle and purse together as follows:
  - Work 2 sts of ruffle tog with 1 st of purse—90 sts. Knit 1 rnd. Do not cut CC2.
- **Inc rnd:** With size 17 needles and 1 strand each of CC1 and Kid Royal held tog, inc in front and back of every st—180 sts.

- Knit 3 rows. BO loosely.
- With size 11 needles, pick up CC2, add a second strand of CC2, and PU 90 sts from joining rnd behind ruffle. Purl 2 rows. BO pw.

Handles (Make 2)

- With dpn and CC2, work 5-st I-cord for 16" (see page 10).
- For firmer handles, insert vinyl tubing into handle before felting. With sharp needle and sewing thread, tack tubing down—sew right through tubing—to prevent it from slipping in felting process. Sew handles in place onto black border of purse, about 3" from corner.

Finishing

- With WS tog, sew bottom seam with whip-stitch.
- Referring to directions on page 8, felt the bag. When felting this piece, form ruffles by pulling them up and down and pinching them.
- **Button loop:** With velour trim, crochet a chain about 2" long and attach on inside of bag along top edge, between black band and ruffle. Sew button in place on opposite side.
- Make 2 bows from velour trim and attach a bow to each side of bag between upper and lower ruffles.

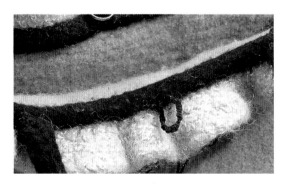

Button closure

This striped bag reminds me of an old-fashioned carpetbag.
The zipper finish gives it a smart—not handmade—look.

Materials

- Cascade 220 (100% wool; 220 yards) in the following colors and amounts:
  - **MC**   2 skeins of Brown
  - **CC**   1 skein each of 4 colors of your choice
- Size 15 US (10 mm) circular needles (24")
- Size 11 US (8 mm) dpn
- Size 10½ US (6.5 mm) dpn
- Size I crochet hook
- Stitch holders
- Separating zipper, 8" long (you may have to cut one to size for your bag)
- Sharp needle and sewing thread to match zipper
- Assorted beads for zipper pull
- Short length of perle cotton for zipper pull

Bag

BEG BAG at bottom. Work 2 strands of yarn held tog throughout.

- With size 15 needles and MC, CO 30 sts. Purl 1 row. *Work 2 rows MC in St st and 2 rows CC in garter st; rep from * 4 times. Work 2 rows MC in St st; purl 1 row.
- Needle CO 60 sts (see "Needle Cast On" on page 11) —90 sts. Join into rnd and purl 1 rnd.
- **Next rnd:** Starting on long side of bottom piece, K30, P15, K30, P15 (knit sts are front and back, and purl sts are sides).
- Cont in patt for 16", using colors in random stripes of 1 to 4 rows of each color.

- **Dec rnd:** Purl 1 rnd, decreasing 4 sts on each long side of bag—82 sts.
- **Next rnd:** K26, BO 15 sts pw, K26 (put sts on holder), BO 15 sts pw.
- Cont on 26 sts; work 8 rows in St st. BO all sts pw.
- With RS facing, join yarn and work 26 sts from holder in St st for 8 rows. BO all sts pw.

Handles (Make 2)

- With size 10½ dpn and MC, work 3-st I-cord for 16 rows (see page 10); put these sts on holder and work another 3-st I-cord for 16 rows.
- With size 11 dpn, join these 2 pieces by working K2, K2tog, K2. Work 5-st I-cord for 10".
- Separate into 2 small I-cords. With 10½ dpn, K2, M1. Put rem sts on holder. Work 3-st I-cord for 16 rows. BO.
- Join yarn to 3 sts on holder. Work 3-st I-cord for 16 rows. BO.

Finishing

- With WS tog, sew bottom piece to CO sts with whipstitch.
- Insert 2 short ends of handle under purl row, at beg of flap, about 4 sts from side and about 2 sts apart, and join ends tog (see page 10); rep with other end of handle. Rep with second handle on opposite side.

- With MC, sc around bag, starting at bottom corner, work up side, across top flap, down other side, across bottom of side, and cont around other side ending at same point you started.

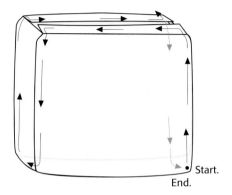

Start.
End.

- Referring to directions on page 8, felt the bag.

NOTE: *To help retain tailored shape, cut out cardboard for bottom and sides and put in bag while it is drying. Happiness is when you find a cardboard box the perfect size.*

- Sew in zipper with regular sewing thread and a sharp needle.
- To make zipper pull, thread beads onto perle cotton and knot the ends to hold the beads. Attach to zipper.

Beaded zipper pull

Golden Basket Tote

I wanted to create a textured tote that looked like a woven basket—I think I got it! I used slip stitches instead of having to carry multiple yarns across.

Materials

- Cascade 220 (100% wool, 220 yards) in the following amounts and colors:
  - 2 skeins of Tan
  - 2 skeins of Light Beige
  - 1 skein of Off-White
  - 1 skein of Dark Brown
- 1 ball of On Line Nobile (75% polyacrylic, 16% metallic, 9% polyester; 99 yards), Gold
- Size 15 US (10 mm) circular needles (24")
- Size 11 US (8 mm) circular needles (24")
- Size 10½ US (6.5 mm) needles
- Grommet kit (you will need a hammer, too) and 6 medium-size grommets
- Purse-magnet closure
- 4" of 1"-wide grosgrain ribbon

Basket Pattern A

Wyib, slip all sts pw.
Rnd 1: With Tan, (K8, sl 2) around.
Rnds 2 and 3: (P8, sl 2) around.
Rnd 4: Change to Light Beige, K3, sl 2, *K8, sl 2, rep from * to last 5 sts, K5.
Rnds 5 and 6: P3, sl 2, *P8, sl 2, rep from * to last 5 sts, P5.
Rnds 7, 8, and 9: Rep rnds 1, 2, and 3 with Tan.

Basket Pattern B

Wyib, slip all sts pw.
Rnd 1: With Light Beige, (K8, sl 2) around.
Rnds 2 and 3: (P8, sl 2) around.
Rnd 4: Change to Tan, K3, sl 2, *K8, sl 2, rep from * to last 5 sts, K5.
Rnds 5 and 6: P3, sl 2, *P8, sl 2, rep from * to last 5 sts, P5.
Rnds 7, 8, and 9: Rep rnds 1, 2, and 3 with Light Beige.

Bag

BEG BAG at top. Work 2 strands of yarn held tog throughout.

- With size 15 needles and Tan, CO 100 sts and join into rnd. Work 4 rnds in garter st (see page 9).
- Knit 2 rnds with Off-White.
- Work basket patt A once.
- Knit 2 rnds with Off-White.
- Work basket patt B once.
- Knit 2 rnds with Off-White.
- Work basket patt A once.
- Knit 2 rnds with Off-White.
- Work basket patt B once.
- Knit 2 rnds with Off-White.
- Work basket patt A once.
- Work rnds 4, 5, and 6 of basket patt A.
- Work basket patt A once.
- **Dec rnd:** With Dark Brown, (K8, K2 tog) around—90 sts. Knit 1 rnd, purl 1 rnd.
- Change to Tan, knit 1 rnd, purl 1 rnd.
- **Dec rnd:** Change to Dark Brown, (K7, K2 tog) around—80 sts. Knit 1 rnd, purl 1 rnd.
- Change to Tan, knit 1 rnd, purl 1 rnd.
- Change to Dark Brown, knit 1 rnd, purl 1 rnd.
- With RS tog, join bottom seam with 3-needle BO (see page 11).
- With size 11 needles, RS facing, and 2 strands of Tan and 1 strand of On Line Nobile held tog, PU 100 sts from top edge. Purl 5 rounds. BO all sts pw.

Handles (Make 2)

WITH SIZE 10½ needles and Dark Brown, CO 5 sts, turn. *K3, sl 2 wyif, turn, rep from * for 32".

Grommets used to attach handles

Magnet closure

Finishing

- ❖ Referring to directions on package, insert grommets about 5" from sides just below rows of Tan and On Line Nobile.
- ❖ Pull one end of a handle through grommet about 4"; fold and sew end to handle. Place grommet through both layers of handle. Rep for opposite end of handle and for second handle on opposite side.
- ❖ Referring to directions on page 8, felt the bag.
- ❖ Attach each half of purse magnet to a 2" length of ribbon.

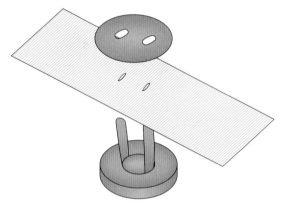

- ❖ With sharp needle and thread, sew ribbon with one-half of magnet to inside of bag at center, about 1" from top edge. Sew ribbon with second half of magnet to opposite side.

Alligator Envelope Bag

This bag was designed for a customer who asked for "a bag that looks like real alligator skin." No problem! I used slip stitches, just as I did in Golden Basket Tote.

FINISHED SIZE AFTER FELTING:
Approx 10" wide x 8½" high

Materials

- 1 skein each of Cascade 220 (100% wool; 220 yards) in the following colors:
  - Light Purple
  - Medium Purple
  - Dark Purple
- 1 ball of Muench Yarn Verikeri (84% nylon, 16% polymide; 113 yards) in Purple Metallic
- Size 15 US (10 mm) circular needles (24")

Bag

BEG BAG at bottom. Work 2 strands of yarn held tog throughout unless otherwise indicated.

- With Dark Purple, CO 90 sts and join into rnd. Purl 3 rnds.
- **Inc rnd:** *K1, inc in next st, (K11, inc in next st) 3 times, P3, inc in next st, P3, rep from * once—100 sts.
- Beg sl st patt (wyib, slip all sts pw):
  - **Rnd 1:** With Light Purple, K1, sl 1, K2, sl 1, K2, sl 1, K3, sl 1, cont working knit and slip sts randomly around.
  - **Rnd 2:** Slip and knit same sts as in rnd 1.
  - **Rnd 3:** With *only 1* strand of Dark Purple, knit all sts.
  - Rep rnds 1, 2, and 3 (slip st rnds with 2 strands and knit rnds with 1 strand) until piece measures 13" to 14". Make sure not to slip the same sts as in the first set so you will create a web-looking design.
- **Dec rnd:** (K8, K2tog) around—90 sts.
- With 2 strands of Dark Purple, purl 3 rnds. BO all sts pw.

Flap

- With 2 strands of Medium Purple and 1 strand of Muench Yarn Verikeri held tog

and RS facing, PU 38 sts from second purl rnd at top.
- Work first and last 2 sts in garter st without Muench Yarn Verikeri, and work sts in between with Muench Yarn Verikeri in reverse St st for 5" (see page 9).
- Dec 1 st at each end inside garter sts, every other row, until 6 sts remain.
- Knit 2 rows. BO all sts kw.

Handle

MAKE A twisted cord (see page 10) about 50" long using 1 strand each of Medium Purple and Muench Yarn Verikeri.

Finishing

- At bottom, with WS tog, fold sides toward inside about ½" to form a small pleat as shown. Sew bottom seam with whipstitch, making sure you catch the edges of the pleat.

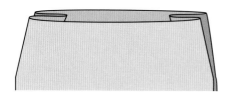

- Insert ends of handle from inside to outside at each side about ½" from top edge. Knot ends of handle on outside of bag.
- Referring to directions on page 8, felt the bag.

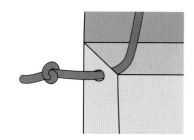

Banana Hobo Bag

The name of this roomy, oblong bag came from its shape. This bag knits up
quickly and requires very little finishing.

FINISHED SIZE AFTER FELTING:
Approx 18" wide x 8½" high

Materials

- **MC** 5 balls of On Line Tondo (100% chunky-weight wool; 50 yards), Light Brown
- **CC1** 1 skein of Cascade 220 (100% wool; 220 yards), Light Orange
- **CC2** 1 ball of Katia Ingenua (78% mohair, 13% nylon, 9% wool; 153 yards), to match CC1
- Size 15 US (10 mm) circular needles (29")
- Stitch holders
- 1 card of Rainbow Gallery Very Velvet Petite, color Orange (thin velour trim)
- Yarn needle
- 1 button, 1" diameter

Bag

BEG BAG at bottom.

- With 1 strand of MC, CO 40 sts. Work 15 rows back and forth in reverse St st (see page 9).
- PU 8 sts along one short end, 40 sts along CO edge, 8 sts along opposite end—96 sts. Join into rnd and work 16 rnds in St st.
- Add CC2 to MC and work 2 rnds.
- Drop MC and add CC1 to CC2; work 2 rnds.
- Drop CC1 and add MC; work 2 rnds.
- Drop CC2 and cont with 1 strand of MC for 6". Put 8 sts from both side ends on holders.
- Work front and back separately. Starting with 40 sts, work dec row: (K2, K2tog) across— 30 sts.
- Change to CC1 and CC2; knit 2 rows, purl 1 row. BO kw. Rep for other side.
- Join 1 strand of MC to 8 sts on holder and work handle as follows:
  - **Row 1:** Sl 1 wyib, K7, turn.
  - **Row 2:** Sl 1 wyif, P7, turn.
  - Rep rows 1 and 2 for 29". Join with Kitchener stitch (see "Seams" on page 10) to the 8 sts on holder.

Finishing

- Referring to directions on page 8, felt the bag.
- With velour trim and yarn needle, whipstitch around both edges of handle.
- Twist together 2 strands of 14"-long velour trim, fold in half, and twist again to make a cord about 7" long for button loop. Insert folded end of cord in center of back just below orange trim at top; pull other end through fold and tighten.
- Sew button on opposite side just below orange trim to correspond with cord. To close, twist cording around button 1 or 2 times.

Whipstitched handle

Button closure

This bag happened by accident. I used a yarn that I thought surely would felt, and without testing it, just knitted the bag. Well, it did not felt. The yarn was Polar by Rowan, which contains 60% wool, 30% alpaca, and 10% acrylic. I did not think that the small amount of acrylic would have such an impact, since the yarn is primarily wool. However, the shape of the bag was so interesting that I made several of them in different colors.

FINISHED SIZE AFTER FELTING:
Approx 17" wide x 12½" high

Materials

- Cascade 220 (100% wool; 220 yards) in the following amounts and colors:
  - 3 skeins Cream
  - 2 skeins Beige
  - 1 skein Light Blue
- 1 skein of any worsted-weight superwash wool (approx 110 yards), White
- 1 ball of Muench Cleo (87% rayon, 13% metal; 62 yards), Cream/Black
- Size 15 US (10 mm) circular needles (29")
- Size 11 US (8 mm) dpn
- 2 buttons, ¾" diameter
- Assorted beads for button loops
- 2 pieces of lightweight elastic, 3" long, from Rainbow Elastic for button loops
- 1 skein of perle cotton for pockets

Queen's Hobo Bag: Pink Flamingo

Bag

BEG BAG at top. Work 2 strands of yarn held tog unless otherwise indicated.

- With size 15 needles and 1 strand each of Cream Cascade and superwash wool held tog, CO 90 sts and join into rnd. Knit 1 rnd, cut Cascade. Cont with superwash wool only, purl 1 rnd, knit 1 rnd. Do not cut yarn.
- **Next rnd:** With 2 strands of Beige Cascade and 1 strand of Muench Cleo held tog, purl 1 rnd.
- **Next rnd:** With 1 strand of superwash, knit 1 rnd.
- Rep last 2 rnds 5 times more.
- **Inc rnd:** With 2 strands of Cream Cascade, (K9, inc 1 st by knitting into front and back of next st) around—100 sts.

Queen's Hobo Bag: Midnight

- Cont in St st, working color sequence as follows:
  - 10 rnds with 2 strands of Cream
  - 7 rnds with 1 strand each of Cream and Beige
  - 3 rnds with 1 strand each of Cream and Light Blue
  - 7 rnds with 1 strand each of Cream and Beige
  - 10 rnds with 2 strands of Cream
  - 4 rnds with 1 strand each of Cream and Beige. (Bag should be approx 16" from beg.)
- With 2 strands of Beige, work 8 rnds in garter st (see page 9).
- **Dec rnd:** K2tog around—50 sts.
- With RS tog, join bottom with 3-needle BO (see page 11).

Handles (Make 2)

WITH dpn and Beige, work 5-st I-cord for 36" (see page 10).

Pocket

- With size 15 needles and 1 strand each of Cream and Muench Cleo held tog, CO 38 sts. Work back and forth in St st for 6".
- Cut Muench Cleo and cont with Cream in garter st for 6 rows. BO all sts pw.

Finishing

- Join ends of handles tog (see page 10). Sew each handle along top edge, measuring 4" from the sides.
- Referring to directions on page 8, felt the bag and pocket.
- Sew pocket in place with perle cotton using a blanket st. Run a backstitch in middle of pocket to divide pocket into 2 sections.
- Thread some beads on 2 strands of elastic thread to make 2 button loops. Sew loops in place at center of each pocket. Sew buttons onto pocket to correspond with loops.

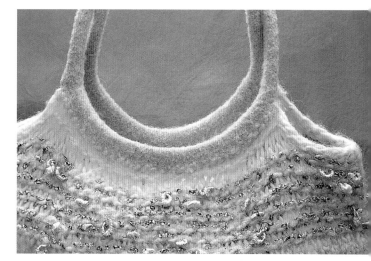

Handles

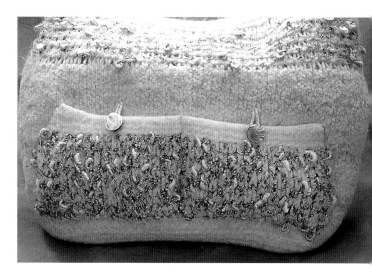

Button closures

My first petite bag is bright, beaded, and cute as a bug!

Materials

- 1 skein each of Cascade 220 (100% wool; 220 yards) in Red and Black
- 1 ball of On Line Nobile (75% polyacrylic, 16% metallic, 9% polyester; 99 yards), Black/Silver
- Size 15 US (10 mm) circular needles (16")
- Size 11 US (8 mm) dpn
- 14 black plastic beads

Bag

BEG BAG at bottom. Work 2 strands of yarn held tog throughout.

- With size 15 needles and Red, CO 50 sts and join into rnd. Knit 1 rnd, purl 1 rnd.
- **Inc rnd:** Inc 1 st in each of next 3 sts by knitting in front and back of st, K22, inc 1 st in each of next 3 sts as before, knit to end of rnd—56 sts.
- Knit 1 rnd, purl 1 rnd.
- Change to Black, knit 1 rnd.
- Change to Red, work in St st for 7".
- **Bead rnd:** (K3, pull next st through bead first and then knit st) around.
- Work another 1" in St st.
- **Dec rnd:** (K5, K2tog) around—48 sts.
- With 2 strands of Black and 1 strand of On Line Nobile held tog, knit 1 rnd, purl 3 rnds. BO all sts pw.

Handles (Make 2)

WITH dpn and Black, work 4-st I-cord for 22" (see page 10).

Finishing

- With WS tog, sew bottom seam with whipstitch.
- Join handles into a circle (see page 10). Starting about 1½" from each side, sew handles to RS of bag at top of bag along third purl row. Then from the inside of the bag, stitch the handles to secure.
- Referring to directions on page 8, felt the bag.

Handles sewn at top of bag

The tailored look of this bag reminds me of an English flannel suit.
It's the perfect accessory to carry in the evening.

Materials

- **MC** 1 skein of Cascade 220 (100% wool; 220 yards), Gray
- **CC1** 2 balls of Cascade Madil (with some wool content; 66 yards), Gray
- **CC2** 1 ball of On Line Nobile (75% poly-acrylic, 16% metallic, 9% polyester; 99 yards), Gray
- Size 15 US (10 mm) circular needles (16")
- Size 11 US (8 mm) needles
- 2 buttons, ¾" diameter

Bag

BEG BAG at bottom. Work 2 strands of yarn held tog throughout.

- With size 15 needles and MC, CO 20 sts. Work 12 rows back and forth in garter st (see page 9).
- Needle CO 40 sts (see page 11)—60 sts. Join into rnd, purl 1 rnd.
- With 1 strand each of MC and CC1 held tog, work as follows:
  - **Next rnd:** Starting on long side of bottom piece,*K20, wyib sl 1 pw, K8, wyib sl 1 pw, rep from * once.
  - **Next rnd:** Knit.
  - Rep last 2 rnds until piece measures 9" from needle CO.
- **Dec rnd:** (K8, K2tog) around—54 sts. Cut CC1.
- With 2 strands MC and 1 strand CC2 held tog, purl 3 rnds. BO all sts pw.

Flap

- With 2 strands of MC and 1 strand of CC2 held tog and RS facing, PU 20 sts from second purl row from back of purse. Work 10 rows in St st.
- Purl 2 rows; work 2 rows in St st.
- Work 2 buttonholes as follows: K3, BO 3, K8, BO 3, K3 (see "One-Row Buttonholes" on page 10).
- Knit 1 row. BO all sts kw.

Handle

- CO 9 sts, turn.
- *K6, wyif sl 3, turn, rep from * for 3".
- K3, K2tog, K1, wyif sl 3, turn.
- *K5, wyif sl 3, turn, rep from * for 2".
- K2, K2tog, K1, wyif sl 3, turn.
- *K4, wyif sl 3, turn, rep from * for 6".
- K2, M1, K2, wyif sl 3, turn.
- *K5, wyif sl 3, turn, rep from * for 2".
- K3, M1, K2, wyif sl 3, turn.
- *K6, wyif sl 3, turn, rep from * for 3". BO all sts.

Finishing

- With WS tog, sew bottom piece to sides with whipstitch.
- Sew each end of handle to top at side edges with 2 strands of MC.
- Referring to directions on page 8, felt the bag. Cut out cardboard shapes to put inside while bag is drying to help maintain shape.
- Sew on buttons to correspond with button-holes.

Handle sewn at side edge

This bag is the all-time favorite with my customers because it is so quick and easy. Express your creativity with your yarn choice— this bag is very adaptable.

Materials

- **MC** 1 skein of Cascade 220 (100% wool; 220 yards). Use 2 skeins of Cascade 220 if the novelty yarn does not contain wool.
- **CC1** 1 ball of On Line Vega (73% wool, 27% acrylic; 77 yards), color to match MC
- **CC2** 1 ball of On Line Nobile (75% poly-acrylic, 16% metallic, 9% polyester; 99 yards), color to match MC
- Size 15 US (10 mm) circular needles (16")
- Size 11 US (8 mm) dpn

Bag

BEG BAG at bottom. Work 2 strands of yarn held tog throughout.

- With size 15 needles and 2 strands of MC, CO 15 sts and work 24 rows in garter st (see page 9).
- PU 15 sts from each remaining side and join into rnd—60 sts. Purl 1 rnd.
- Cut 1 strand of MC, add 1 strand of CC1, knit for 8". Or continue with 2 strands MC, adding other kinds of novelty yarns as desired.
- **Dec rnd:** (K8, K2tog) around—54 sts.
- Cut CC1, add 1 strand of CC2, purl 3 rnds. BO all sts pw.

Handle

WITH dpn and 2 strands of MC and 1 strand CC2 held tog, work 3-st I-cord for 34" (see page 10).

Finishing

- Starting about 4 sts from corners, thread handle in and out as shown below; rep on opposite side. Join ends tog (see page 10).
- Referring to directions on page 8, felt the bag. Move handle back and forth during felting so it does not felt in place. Handle can be worn long when pulled to one side, or short when pulled from both ends.

Handle threaded through edges of bag

This elegant little evening bag is a classic.

Materials

- 2 skeins of Cascade 220 (100% wool; 220 yards), Black
- 1 ball On Line Nobile (75% polyacrylic, 16% metallic, 9% polyester; 99 yards), Black Metallic
- Size 15 US (10 mm) circular needles (16")
- Size 10½ US (6.5 mm) dpn
- Size I crochet hook
- 1 button, ⅞" diameter

Bag

BEG BAG at bottom. Work 2 strands of yarn held tog throughout.

- With size 15 needles and Black, CO 62 sts and join into rnd.
- Work patt for 8" as follows: K25, P6, K25, P6.
- **Dec rnd:** (P8, P2tog) around to last 12 sts, end P10, P2tog—56 sts.
- Purl 1 rnd. BO all sts pw.

Flap

- Add 1 strand of On Line Nobile to the 2 strands of Black and with RS facing, PU 23 sts from back of purse at second purl row from top.
- Work in reverse St st for 6". BO all sts kw.

Handle

WITH dpn and 1 strand each of Black and On Line Nobile held tog, work 5-st I-cord for 36" (see page 10).

Finishing

- At bottom, with WS tog, fold sides toward inside about ½" to form a small pleat (see "Finishing" on page 44). Sew bottom seam with whipstitch, making sure you catch the edges of the pleat.
- With 2 strands of Black, sc around sides and flap. Start at top of one side just below purl rnds, work down side, across bottom of side, up other side. Cont around flap, making a 10-chain buttonhole loop at center of flap. Cont down other side, across bottom of side, and up side, ending just below purl rnds near top.

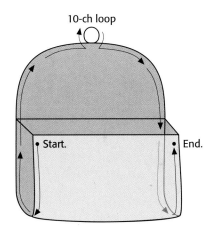

10-ch loop
Start.
End.

- Insert each end of handle from inside to outside at sides, about ¾" from top edge; knot ends of handle on outside of bag.

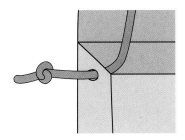

- Referring to directions on page 8, felt the bag.
- Sew on button to correspond with button loop.

Large Travel Tote

This tote will use up all your leftover wool and novelty yarn scraps!
Just pick two or three base colors to tie all the colors together.

Materials

- Approx 7 to 8 skeins of Cascade 220 (100% wool; 220 yards) in various colors
- Assorted novelty yarns
- Size 15 US (10 mm) circular needles (29")
- Size 11 US (8 mm) needles
- Separating zipper, 16" long (measure for zipper after bag is felted)
- Sharp needle and sewing thread to match zipper
- 1 skein of perle cotton for pockets
- 2 buttons, 1" diameter

Bag

BEG BAG at bottom. Work 2 strands of yarn held tog throughout.

- With size 15 needles, CO 54 sts. *Knit 3 rows, purl 1 row, rep from * 8 times. Knit 3 rows.
- PU 32 sts along one narrow end, 54 sts along CO edge, and 32 sts along opposite narrow end and join into rnd—172 sts. Work in St st until piece measures 20" from PU row, changing colors and textures as desired.
- **Dec rnd:** (K9, K2tog) around to last 9 sts, end K7, K2tog—156 sts.
- Work 8 rnds in garter st (see page 9).
- **Top edge:** *P49, (P1, K1, P1) in next st, P27, (P1, K1, P1) in next st, rep from * once—164 sts.
- Purl 3 rnds. BO pw, purling 3 sts tog at each corner (where you inc sts)—156 sts.
- **Bottom edge:** With RS facing and bottom facing up, PU 32 sts from each short end, and 45 sts from each long side of bag—154 sts. Join into rnd, [(P1, K1, P1) in first st,

P30, (P1, K1, P1) in next st, P45] twice— 162 sts. Purl 3 rnds. BO all sts pw, purling 3 sts tog in each corner.

Flaps

- With RS facing, PU 49 sts from first row inside top edge along long side of bag. Work in St st, inc 1 st at each end EOR 8 times— 65 sts.
- Knit 2 rows. BO all sts kw. Work opposite long side in same manner.
- Sew about 1" of flap ends tog. PU 8 sts from each end for button flaps. Work 16 rows in garter st. Make buttonhole as follows: K2, BO 4, K2 (see "One-Row Buttonholes" on page 10). Knit 2 rows. Dec 1 st at each end EOR 3 times. BO remaining sts.

Handles (Make 2)

- With size 11 needles, CO 2 sts. Knit 2 rows. Work in garter st, inc 1 st at each end EOR 3 times—8 sts. Knit 2 rows.
- **Next row:** K3, K2tog, wyif sl 3 sts, turn— 7 sts.
- *K4, wyif slip 3 sts, turn, rep from * for 20".
- Inc 1 st in middle of row—8 sts. Knit 2 rows.
- Dec 1 st at each end EOR 3 times—2 sts. Knit 2 rows. BO.

Pockets (Make 2)

FOR EACH pocket, use size 15 needles and CO 30 sts. Work in St st, ending with 6 rows garter st until pocket measures 16". BO all sts kw.

Finishing

- Sew each end handle to RS of bag just below garter-st border at top, about 6" from corners. Rep with second handle on opposite side.
- Referring to directions on page 8, felt the bag and pockets.
- Sew pockets to sides of bag with perle cotton using blanket st.
- Sew zipper into flap with regular sewing thread and a sharp needle.
- Sew a button to top of each pocket.

Zipper and button flap

Handle sewn below garter-st border

Abbreviations

approx	approximately		**P2tog**	purl two stitches together
beg	begin, beginning		**patt**	pattern
BO	bind off		**PU**	pick up and knit
CC	contrasting color		**PM**	place marker
ch	chain		**pw**	purlwise
CO	cast on		**rem**	remaining
cont	continue		**rep**	repeat
dec	decrease		**rnd**	round
dpn	double-pointed needles		**RS**	right side(s)
EOR	every other row		**sc**	single crochet
inc	increase		**sl**	slip
K	knit		**st(s)**	stitch(es)
K2tog	knit two stitches together		**St st**	stockinette stitch
kw	knitwise		**tog**	together
M1	make one stitch		**WS**	wrong side(s)
MC	main color		**wyib**	with yarn in back
P	purl		**wyif**	with yarn in front

Resources

THE SUPPLIES and accessories used for the purses in this book should be available at your local yarn shop, craft store, or hardware store. If you can't find any of these items, please contact Eva at her shop.

Eva's Needlework
1321 E. Thousand Oaks Blvd., #120
Thousand Oaks, CA 91362
805-379-0722

and a 17-year stopover in Germany, she came to America with her husband and daughter in 1984. Since 1987, she has been the owner of Eva's Needlework in Thousand Oaks, California.

At Eva's shop, every knitter and needleworker can feel at home. The excitement is catching when you walk into this store packed with yarn. Eva's Needlework was featured in a knitting publication as one of America's premiere shops, which made Eva and her loyal customers very proud.

Eva Wiechmann was born in Finland, a country of long, cold winters and summers with midnight sun. Eva learned to knit and crochet at the age of four. After graduating from school

New and Bestselling Titles from

America's Best-Loved Craft & Hobby Books®
America's Best-Loved Knitting Books®

America's Best-Loved Quilt Books®

NEW RELEASES
300 Paper-Pieced Quilt Blocks
American Doll Quilts
Classic Crocheted Vests
Dazzling Knits
Follow-the-Line Quilting Designs
Growing Up with Quilts
Hooked on Triangles
Knitting with Hand-Dyed Yarns
Lavish Lace
Layer by Layer
Lickety-Split Quilts
Magic of Quiltmaking, The
More Nickel Quilts
More Reversible Quilts
No-Sweat Flannel Quilts
One-of-a-Kind Quilt Labels
Patchwork Showcase
Pieced to Fit
Pillow Party!
Pursenalities
Quilter's Bounty
Quilting with My Sister
Seasonal Quilts Using Quick Bias
Two-Block Appliqué Quilts
Ultimate Knitted Tee, The
Vintage Workshop, The
WOW! Wool-on-Wool Folk Art Quilts

APPLIQUÉ
Appliquilt in the Cabin
Blossoms in Winter
Garden Party
Shadow Appliqué
Stitch and Split Appliqué
Sunbonnet Sue All through the Year

HOLIDAY QUILTS & CRAFTS
Christmas Cats and Dogs
Christmas Delights
Hocus Pocus!
Make Room for Christmas Quilts
Welcome to the North Pole

LEARNING TO QUILT
101 Fabulous Rotary-Cut Quilts
Happy Endings, Revised Edition
Loving Stitches, Revised Edition
More Fat Quarter Quilts
Quilter's Quick Reference Guide, The
Sensational Settings, Revised Edition
Simple Joys of Quilting, The
Your First Quilt Book (or it should be!)

PAPER PIECING
40 Bright and Bold Paper-Pieced Blocks
50 Fabulous Paper-Pieced Stars
Down in the Valley
Easy Machine Paper Piecing
For the Birds
Papers for Foundation Piecing
Quilter's Ark, A
Show Me How to Paper Piece
Traditional Quilts to Paper Piece

QUILTS FOR BABIES & CHILDREN
Easy Paper-Pieced Baby Quilts
Easy Paper-Pieced Miniatures
Even More Quilts for Baby
More Quilts for Baby
Quilts for Baby
Sweet and Simple Baby Quilts

ROTARY CUTTING/SPEED PIECING
365 Quilt Blocks a Year Perpetual
   Calendar
1000 Great Quilt Blocks
Burgoyne Surrounded
Clever Quarters
Clever Quilts Encore
Endless Stars
Once More around the Block
Pairing Up
Stack a New Deck
Star-Studded Quilts
Strips and Strings
Triangle-Free Quilts

SCRAP QUILTS
Easy Stash Quilts
Nickel Quilts
Rich Traditions
Scrap Frenzy
Successful Scrap Quilts

TOPICS IN QUILTMAKING
Asian Elegance
Batiks and Beyond
Bed and Breakfast Quilts
Coffee-Time Quilts
Dutch Treat
English Cottage Quilts
Fast-Forward Your Quilting
Machine-Embroidered Quilts
Mad about Plaid!
Romantic Quilts
Simple Blessings

CRAFTS
20 Decorated Baskets
Beaded Elegance
Blissful Bath, The
Collage Cards
Creating with Paint
Holidays at Home
Pretty and Posh
Purely Primitive
Stamp in Color
Trashformations
Warm Up to Wool
Year of Cats…in Hats!, A

KNITTING & CROCHET
365 Knitting Stitches a Year Perpetual
   Calendar
Beyond Wool
Classic Knitted Vests
Crocheted Aran Sweaters
Crocheted Lace
Crocheted Socks!
Garden Stroll, A
Knit it Now!
Knits for Children and Their Teddies
Knits from the Heart
Knitted Throws and More
Knitter's Template, A
Little Box of Scarves, The
Little Box of Sweaters, The
Style at Large
Today's Crochet
Too Cute! Cotton Knits for Toddlers

Our books are available at bookstores and your favorite craft, fabric, and yarn retailers. If you don't see the title you're looking for, visit us at
www.martingale-pub.com
or contact us at:
1-800-426-3126

International: 1-425-483-3313
Fax: 1-425-486-7596
Email: info@martingale-pub.com